Table of Contents

How purpose-driven people think differently to achieve unconventional success in life and business. 4

INTRODUCTION 5

So, who am I and why should you care? 8

What are the Top 7 Killer Success Secrets of Incredibly Successful People? 11

Here's what you'll discover... 11

How to use the Top 7 Killer Success Secrets 16

Secret #1: 7 Keys to Killer Communication Skills .. 19

Key #1: It's not about you 21

Key #2: Be transparent 23

Key #3: Listen actively 25

Active listening requires you to do 3 things: 26

Key #4: Say what you mean 27

Key #5: Be responsible 29

Key #6: Value accountability 32

Key #7: Know when to shut up 35

Secret #2: 7 Steps to Killer Networking Skills 38

Step #1: Be proactive 41

Step #2: Study the landscape 42

Step #3: Act with purpose 44

Step #4: Seek to help 45

Step #5: Keep your word 47

Step #6: Stay in touch 49

Step #7: Ask for help 52

Secret #3: 7 Steps to Killer Negotiation 55

Step #1: Know What You Want 58

Step #2: Foresight is better Than Hindsight 60

Step #3: Sit On the Same Side 61

Step #4: Understand What They Want First 63

Step #5: Reveal Your Vision 65

Step #6: The Third Alternative 67

Step #7: No Deal is better Than a Raw Deal 68

Do YOU Have What It Takes to Become an Effective Negotiator? 70

Secret #4: 7 Steps to Building a Killer Team 72

Step #1: Embody the mission 75

Step #2: Cultivate Synergy 86

Step #3: Level the playing field 90

Step #4: Foster heretics 92

Step #5: Discourage conformists 94

Step #6: Be A Square 97

Step #7: Get out of the way 100

What kind of team are you on? 104

Secret #5: 7 Ways to Add Killer Value to Anything 105

Way #1: Bigger 108

1

    Way #2: Better 109

    Way #3 – Faster 110

    Way #4 – Innovate 111

    Way #5 – Exclusivity 112

    Way #6 – Personality 113

    Way #7 – Relatable 114

    Here's the skinny… 116

Secret #6: Top 7 Sales Killers 118

    Sales Killer #1: Assumption 120

    Sales Killer #2: Cluelessness 121

    Sales Killer #3: Judgment 122

    Sales Killer #4: Insincerity 123

    Sales Killer #5: Indifference 124

    Sales Killer #6: Dishonesty 125

    Sales Killer #7: Doubt 127

    There you have it… 128

Secret #7: 7 Steps to Killer Success 129

    Step #1: Start at the finish line 131

    Step #2: Draw the correct map 134

    Step #3: Employ the 4 quadrants 136

    Step #4: Spread the wealth 138

    Step #5: Pay it forward 140

    Step #6: Value Principles 142

    Step #7: Do what you love 143

So, What Now? 147

THE TOP 7 KILLER SUCCESS SECRETS OF INCREDIBLY SUCCESSFUL PEOPLE

How purpose-driven people think differently to achieve unconventional success in life and business.

INTRODUCTION

The truth is that there is no real *"secret"* to what I am about to share with you – just awareness or in some cases, the lack thereof. Everything I am about to reveal in this book, you either know about or heard about BUT probably not using it all properly or at the right times.

Look, if you're reading this, it means that you demand more than average performance from yourself; and you're no Neanderthal.

You're at the very least smart enough to know that you do need to do something different to get you where you want to go. And what better way to get where you want to go than to simply duplicate what the most successful people do.

One of my mentors used to say **"Dean, if you want to be successful, find someone else who is already successful at what you want to do and follow him or her."**

How hard can that be?

The point is, I didn't come up with this concept on my own – I am duplicating what another successful individual did. Yes, the content is all original – my take; however, the concept is as old as the universe... no reinvention of the wheel here.

Now, I am not naïve, and I trust neither are you...

What you are about to discover is by no means easy to stick with; however, it is simple and more importantly very doable. As long as you're serious and as we've established before – you're not a Neanderthal.

Here's the deal...

If you are seriously ready to make a profound, positive, and significant leap in your success, keep reading. Reserve your judgments and make sure you diligently try everything you discover.

The bottom line is that one of the reasons people continue to fail is because they don't believe something is going to work and they refuse to stick with the program.

While true success takes very simple steps; sticking to the script is hard work so make sure you're really ready. Besides, if it were easy to stick with it – everyone would do it.

Nothing worth having comes easy – you've got to pay the price – NO EXCEPTIONS!

So, who am I and why should you care?

One of my great teachers would always say **"before you presume to lead others in anything, you must earn the right."**

That's what I am going to do here because quite frankly I am a stickler for only seeking advice and leadership from qualified people.

You should make sure you always do the same… too often we solicit the wrong people for advice and then wonder why we end up worse off than we were in the first place.

My name is Dean Forbes and I have been training and developing leaders for over 17 years, as of the publishing of this book.

I've been mentored by some of the greatest minds of the past half century, and I've coached thousands of people from all walks of life.

From the lessons I've learned to the hard-won battles I've encountered; I've dedicated my life to always making an impact that matters.

I have not only studied and learned from the best in leadership, business, and life – I have personally applied the knowledge I've acquired to my own life, and I am living proof that these successful principles work.

I have coached and mentored thousands of creative business owners and savvy professionals that have gone on to achieve amazing breakthrough results in their businesses, careers, and personal lives.

All this is to say that if they can do it, you can do it. And, if I can do it, you can certainly do it. What I wouldn't say is that ANYONE can do it, because you and I both know that you're in the minority.

Consistently pursuing excellence within oneself is rare, and we both know it.

The good news is that you're in great company so let's dig in and get right to it.

What are the Top 7 Killer Success Secrets of Incredibly Successful People?

The **Top 7 Killer Success Secrets of Incredibly Successful People** consist of a series of **7** blueprints focused on achieving highly effective results. While there are so many other angles and schools of thought to achieving success – these **7** blueprints have the most comprehensive and relevant principles you need to catapult your personal life and business.

There are lots of little ways to move the needle of success; however, I trust that you're reading this because you are ready to make a quantum leap in your life, and business. If that's the case, time to stop chomping on the kibbles and bits, and start playing where the big dogs play.

Here's what you'll discover…

Secret #1: 7 Keys to Killer Communication Skills

If you can't communicate your message effectively, you'll be hard-pressed to move the needle of success. Discover how to develop and significantly improve what I believe is one of the most important human skill you could ever hope to master.

Secret #2: 7 Steps to Killer Networking Skills

It really is true that people make the world go round. If you can't cultivate and nurture a successful network, failure is certain. No man or woman is an island – we all need others to achieve greatness and that's the way it's supposed to be. The pinnacle of excellence is not independence but interdependence. Discover the killer art of networking from the minds of the masters.

Secret #3: 7 Steps to Killer Negotiation

The fine art of negotiation is integral to your success and the most successful people are masters in this arena. Discover the true essence of how to negotiate and achieve win/win solutions in almost every single situation, both personal and professional.

Secret #4: 7 Steps to Building a Killer Team

Let's face it: you're either on the team that gets killed or the one making the killing. Where would you rather be? Killer Teams aren't necessarily the ones with all the badges and gold stars; however, they are always the ones who make the most impactful difference in the world around them. Get inside the minds of championship teams and discover how to transform ordinary people into extraordinary teams.

Secret #5: 7 Ways to Add Killer Value to Anything

Success demands that you find ways to create and deliver value for others. No matter what you do or what you sell, if others don't want your services or need your goods, you might as well close up shop. Find out the 7 ways you can make your service and/or product much more appealing to others.

Secret #6: Top 7 Sales Killers

Whether you're selling services, products or just yourself – we are all salespeople whether we like it or not. That means that it is imperative that you understand what elements instantly kill a sale so you can avoid the pitfalls of the vast majority. Mastering the art of the killer sale isn't just for *"salespeople"*; it's for everyone because we are all selling something to someone, even our spouses when we plan date night or buy a gift.

Secret #7: 7 Steps to Killer Success

The point of this one is obvious; it ties all the others together in a nice and neat package. The **7 Steps to Killer Success** is essentially a blueprint to the mindset of the most incredibly successful people. Perhaps I should have started with this one; ultimately, I left it for last. Whatever, as long as it's here; first – last – makes no difference. Just make sure you get into it and apply what you discover.

How to use the Top 7 Killer Success Secrets

Before you jump in or jump around…

…for maximum effect I want to provide a few tips on how to use this incredible master blueprint. If you're like me you've probably already skimmed over this section – yes – I do skim a lot before I dive into something.

If you're reading this section however, great, you just saved yourself a lot of time.

The main reason I outlined what is inside this master blueprint in the previous chapter was to give you an overview of what you are getting. This way you can plan accordingly.

Here are 7 tips to get you started quickly…

1. Don't try to digest it all at once; do it in bite sized pieces

2. Start with the success secret you truly believe you need to work on the most and work your way through them all in the order of greatest need
3. Try mastering each success secret one at a time – the more you practice the better your results will get
4. Apply each success secret in your personal and business circles every chance you get
5. Make it a point to teach others what you've learned to help you retain the information and concepts much more quickly
6. When you're through with all the success secrets – just go back to the beginning and repeat
7. Please refer others to this incredible material if you believe in it – send your friends and colleagues the amazon link so they too can experience its power.

Whether you are a veteran or a beginner, these insights can help you significantly improve the results you achieve and increase your success rate tremendously.

ARE YOU GAME?

Secret #1: 7 Keys to Killer Communication Skills

No matter who you are or what you do, if you don't learn how to communicate effectively, the quality of your life will suffer. This is a fact!

I say that because through my training and experience over the years, I have discovered that the quality of my communication ultimately determines the quality of my life. The more effective you are at getting your message across to others, the better the results you will yield.

The clarity and quality of your written, verbal, and visual communication will always have a tremendous impact on your ability to achieve the results you desire.

It is extremely important that you grasp this concept sooner rather than later so that you can begin putting the correct communication principles into practice.

If you find that you are constantly having to answer the same questions or repeatedly clarifying your position – there is clearly an issue with your communication.

Understanding the elements of effective communication and applying them religiously will undoubtedly increase your ability to consistently achieve your goals.

Now that I have raised your awareness to this crucial element of your personal growth – here's the good news. It's not rocket science by any stretch; you have the ability to discover, learn and apply the principles of killer communication skills that will ultimately help you to consistently achieve the results YOU desire.

Following are my best insights on becoming a killer communicator; these are the **7 Keys to Killer Communication Skills.**

Key #1: It's not about you

All killer communicators understand that the most important person in any line of communication is the person receiving the message. This means that you must relay your message in a manner that is easy to understand by the receiving parties.

Your focus when you are the messenger has to be on the needs of your audience; what's in it for them. This is a good way to ensure that what is heard is received as you intended.

Too often, we forget that communication is about others thereby putting way too much emphasis on ourselves and our needs. What usually happens in cases such as these is we lose the audience, and the intended message gets skewed.

Whenever you are ready to put a message together, think first about the receiving party; imagine you are in his or her shoes and compose your message so that it relates to him or her on a familiar level.

If you are communicating with someone for the first time, the best thing you can do is ask questions that help you discover the best communication style or method for this person. Not everyone receives information in the same way or at the same speed – different strokes for different folks.

Additionally, be sure to remove your ego from the equation when you communicate with others – *it's not about you*. Unless you grasp this simple concept, your ego will continue to get the best of you and your communications will often go awry. You cannot develop killer communication skills unless you put others first.

Key #2: Be transparent

This is a crucial element in developing your communication skills. You must be upfront about your objectives and expectations. Are you simply disseminating information or are you asking for something? You must be clear about the results you want and your motives.

Killer communicators know that it is imperative that goals are clear to all parties in the line of communication. Each link in the chain must be crystal clear on what is expected, otherwise, your ends will not be met.

Transparent communication demands that there are no hidden agendas. If there are things that will come to light later that your audience does not need to know at the time of your communication – by all means say so.

Some scholars may disagree with me on this point; however, in my experience I have never known transparency to hamper or erode my communications with others. I have also not known it to impede or damage the desired results. In fact, I have always found that the desired result is achieved with more efficacy and speed.

People commit more quickly and are more accountable when they know the deal upfront. People value honesty and so should you when you communicate. If there are things that you are not at liberty to say – be sure to let your audience know that.

The most important thing for them is that they know you value and respect them. Transparency earns you the right to speak to your audience and have them reciprocate with action.

You have no idea how powerful this practice can be until you've tried it – you will see immediate and positive results.

Key #3: Listen actively

Active listening requires first that you genuinely want to hear what the receiving party has to say. When you communicate with others it is vital that you understand that they have understood your message and what actions to take next. This means that you have to ask for clarification and then listen – truly listen – to the response.

All killer communicators are active listeners. They acknowledge others' concerns and take the necessary steps to overcome any objections. When you listen actively, you are not only listening to what is being said but also to what is not. This is why it is important that your heart and mind are open to hearing the message coming back at you.

The goal of active listening is to clear up misunderstandings and clarify action steps and expectations. This is an element you do not want to skip when you communicate because if there are any misunderstandings, they will undoubtedly surface in the results you achieve.

The same is true for confusion about what to do next and expectations; if your audience is not clear on this, how will they make the right decisions – take the appropriate actions?

Active listening requires you to do 3 things:

1. Deliver your message and then ask your audience if it makes sense – if they are clear
2. Listen to the response you get – listen with an open heart and mind – be genuine
3. Respond by overcoming any objections and/or clarifying next steps and expectations – then go back to #1 and repeat until you are all on the same page

Chances are very good that if you follow this process, you won't have to repeat it often before clarity is achieved.

Key #4: Say what you mean

Say what you mean to say – don't dance. When you beat around the bush, you leave way too much room for error and confusion. Killer communicators don't dance unless they are at a party.

Don't be afraid to say exactly what you mean. You don't have to be a jerk about it when what you mean to say might be deemed as ugly; however, as sensitively as you can, you still need to spell it out. Don't mince words with your audience if you want to be a killer communicator.

Surely, there is a certain amount of finesse that comes with delivering ugly messages without making them sound so ugly. Lead with compassion and tact. You will never be able to please everyone so just stick to what's true for you and learn to live with the consequences. Besides, if everyone you know agrees with everything you say and do, one of you is lying.

It is always better to lay it on the table as it is or as you see it than to make stuff up. When you manufacture words and add fluff, the real message is stifled which means your results will suffer the same fate.

Your best course to success is to simply say what you mean to say. If need be, just ask your audience for permission to be brutally honest. This way it shows that you care about and value them. It seems like an easy thing; however, in my experience this is one of the hardest things for many people to do.

Yes, it is a simple concept to grasp – just a hard discipline to master. Once you are able to do it though, your communication skills will improve drastically.

Key #5: Be responsible

One of the worse things you can do as a communicator is to be irresponsible for what you say. Killer communicators live by the code "**the buck stops here**." You must be responsible for your words – don't pass the buck to the other guy.

One of my mentors and friend, Chris, taught me that *"communication is the response you get."* Simply put, it is your responsibility as a killer communicator to make sure that your audience receives your message in a clear and succinct manner. You are responsible for the message you deliver and also whether or not it is understood.

If for whatever reason the results are not what you expect, the responsibility of those results is yours. You do not pass the buck to the person who misunderstood or who was confused about next steps and expectations. If you had done your job of communicating effectively, the results would have been different – more to your liking. If they are not, you obviously missed a step, and you need to go back and fix it.

I know it can be hard not to think… how can I control what someone else does? Obviously, you can't but that's not the point. The point is that if you want to be a killer communicator, learn to accept the fact that the buck must stop with you.

If for some reason you are unable to reach someone in your communication or the person refuses to be open to your message, then you have the right to decide to stop communicating with this person.

Furthermore, you can always reduce your expectations of others without lowering your standards. You do not blame others for miscommunication when you delivered the message no matter what. You always look at you and then decide how best to proceed.

Is it still a bit much to swallow? Let me put it another way.

If you were training a dog to guard your home and each time you gave the attack command, the dog simply rolled over and went to sleep. How long would you continue to train that dog before you got rid of him?

Sure, you could sit around all day blaming the dog for being a no good mutt, but you still wouldn't have a guard dog.

Are you getting the picture? Good – let's move on.

Key #6: Value accountability

All killer communicators understand that effective communication requires accountability from those receiving your message. As long as you are practicing all the keys, there is no reason you should not expect audience accountability. This is of high value when it comes to improving your communication skills.

Whether your audience has to act or not, their accountability lies in the expectations that you have agreed upon between communicator and audience. If your job as the communicator is to be responsible, then it is the job of your audience to be accountable and to expect you to hold them to it.

Of course, you cannot force anyone to be accountable – your goal is simply to be able to call people out when they are not. Notice that I didn't say embarrass – agreements allow you to remind others (gently) of what you agreed to. This is how you decide where to focus your energies so that you neither waste other peoples' time nor yours.

A major reason why so many people spin their wheels when communicating is that they continue to communicate with the same (wrong) people and expect to achieve a different result. This is insanity and it drives people nuts.

Even if you are communicating (presenting) to a large group – 10 or more – I have found it easiest to just ask for accountability. Based on the nature of the presentation and the way you set it up in your introduction, you can simply ask them if they are willing to play.

Once they've agreed, you will have no trouble reminding them of the rules of the game and garnering compliance.

For example, back when I conducted sales meetings, I would always ask my audience to silence their phones, play full out and ask questions when they don't understand something. Once I asked that, I would then enroll them with one simple request... by a show of hands, how many of you are willing to play?

Inevitably, they would all raise their hands and inevitably by the end of the meeting someone would test the lines to violate one of the ground rules like answering the phone or engaging in a sidebar conversation.

Because they agreed to the rules of engagement, I would simple and gently remind them of that agreement and it would fix the problem instantly – well 99% of the time.

Value accountability and have the courage to hold people to it once they've agreed. Effective communication requires – demands – accountability from the receiving party and all killer communicators know it.

Key #7: Know when to shut up

There are so many clichés that I can use here to drive this point home. I have heard before "*Why do you think that God gave you two ears and one mouth?*" I have also heard "*Sometimes it is better to be thought of as a fool than to open your mouth and remove all doubt.*" Yup, my dad is a wise man.

Both of these really sum up the point of not only why it is important to listen but also when to be silent. I still have a battle with myself every now and then with this practice. (Chuckles)

But seriously…

Knowing when to shut up is vital to improving your communication skills. Often times because of assumptions and preconceptions, we do not shut up long enough to give others a chance to respond to us. We tend to want to answer for them.

Killer communicators are masters at knowing when silence is golden, and they practice this discipline religiously. The best insight I can offer on this is to simply pause and give others a chance to steal the thunder. Believe me; other people want to hear themselves talk just as much as you do.

Besides, the more you let others talk, the more you will learn if you are listening actively. This will help you make wiser decisions about your communication with others.

So, in a nutshell – learn to shut up – let others talk – it's not about you – it's about them – so just throw them the ball and open up your heart and mind like a big hoop.

Quick FAQ

Whenever I have delivered this presentation or talked with others about how to become highly effective communicators, I always get this question.

Q. Dean, can anyone become a highly effective communicator?

I'm going to answer that question here for you because I know it bubbles to the surface often.

Here's the deal...

- A. The short answer is NO – not anyone can become a highly effective communicator; however, I believe that most intelligent and open-minded people can. Unfortunately, we are in short supply of that species on this planet. I dare you – NO I double dare you to take the challenge!

Secret #2: 7 Steps to Killer Networking Skills

Networking has long been one of the most important things you can do to increase your visibility and influence. Individuals who have developed strong networks tend to almost always get ahead faster and more efficiently than those who do not.

Sure, it takes more than a strong network to achieve at high levels; however, a strong network provides a lot more opportunities for you to make your mark. In fact, while book-smarts can often be very important in your success – it is much more difficult to hit your goals without a strong network.

On the other hand, if you have a strong network – you can succeed at the highest levels even without book-smarts. That, I guess, makes *Killer Networking* more like **street-smarts**.

In my experience, having a strong network has proven to be one of the most crucial elements in my success. I give great credit to where I am now to the incredible network that I have been able to develop and continue to cultivate.

A very significant part of my pursuit of personal growth and excellence includes killer networking. Developing this skill, I believe, is absolutely necessary for you to achieve at the highest levels.

When I was only 25 years old, armed with nothing but an Associates Degree in Business from a community college, I landed my first six-figure job on Wall Street. Yup, that's right. At the ripe old age of 25, I was working in one of the most coveted places by career professionals alongside MBAs and Ivy Leaguers.

That accomplishment in large part I attribute to the network I had built to that point. So, umm, yeah, I'd say this is a crucial skill to your ultimate success.

Following are the **7 Steps to Killer Networking Skills** that once mastered will undoubtedly help you improve in your personal growth and rapidly move the needle closer to your goals.

Step #1: Be proactive

The first rule of thumb in networking is that you have to do something; nothing happens unless you make it happen. Sitting around and hoping that you get the opportunity to meet the right people at the right time is a fool's folly.

The very core of networking is that you are constantly in the mode of connecting with others. If you are not moving towards others, you're not truly seeking to expand your circle.

To be proactive as a skilled networker means that you understand that you are 100% responsible for taking the steps necessary to make meaningful connections. Individuals with highly developed skills in this art are always seeking to collaborate with others who are going somewhere – adding value – doing things that make a difference.

So, in a nutshell – get off your ass-ets and do something.

Step #2: Study the landscape

While you are being proactive, it is crucially important to know with whom you are dealing. Whenever you seek to network with others, it is important that you understand who they are and what they are about. Simply stepping into the arena and not knowing your audience always proves to be an amateur's move.

Studying the landscape will ensure that you know just what makes the people you seek to connect with, tick. At the very least, you should understand their interests and know their accomplishments.

Also, it is a very good idea to look for commonalities either in personality or experiences. The bottom line is it can only help you if you can decipher different ways, you can actually connect with others in a meaningful way.

When I say study the landscape – I don't mean for manipulative purposes. What I mean is that once you know your audience, you can find truly authentic and more impactful ways of making a connection.

Killer networkers are avid researchers; they are constantly looking for common ground on which to play with others. The fact is that they understand that the more relative and level you can make the playing field, the greater your chances of hitting a home run in the **networking** arena.

So, do your homework before you dive into the vast ocean to play with the big fishes.

Step #3: Act with purpose

When it comes to networking, *Killer Networkers* only move with a mission. They know precisely these 4 things:

    a. What they are going to do
    b. Why they are going to do it
    c. How they are going to do it
    d. When they are going to do it

There are no accidents in the purpose-driven life of killer networkers. Acting with purpose means that unless you have a plan for the connection you seek to make – you don't move on it.

Certainly, there are times when things will happen spontaneously; however, these moments are the exception and not the rule. At times like that you simply act in a manner that feels right to you and live with the consequences of your actions. Besides, you're not simply giving to get – you're just being a good human being.

So, don't move unless you can answer the 4 questions above and then put some pep in your step.

Step #4: Seek to help

This is one the most missed principles in the art of killer networking. Killer networkers truly believe in helping others. In fact, it is the nucleus of why they network in the first place. They are always looking to make an impact that matters.

Sure, there is a very public agenda to advance in your own dreams and goals; however, there is a clear understanding of how powerful it is when you simply help others achieve their dreams and goals.

Killer Networking requires that you genuinely seek to help others. That means that you deliberately seek to understand the desires of others and then apply your true gifts and talents to help them achieve the results they desire.

Most people, when they attend a networking event, go with one purpose – to hand out as many business cards as possible and talk about how great they are. This is utterly useless – not to mention obnoxious. Does anyone else find this person annoying or is it just me?

If you truly want to improve your networking skills – take it to the highest level – seek to genuinely help others achieve their desired results. Find ways to be of great value to others and they will never forget you for that. More often than not, they become your biggest cheerleaders.

The networkers who only talk about themselves and their perceived greatness come off as the type who don't need cheerleaders because they've already got it all. No one needs to talk about these people because according to them they are all set – **NOT!**

So, remember, killer networkers truly seek to help others achieve their dreams and goals first. And, in return, and without expectation they reap much greater rewards.

Step #5: Keep your word

This is so important! The truth is that this is not only the quickest and most effective way to grow your influence – not doing it is the quickest way to shrink your circle. All killer networkers know that it is imperative that they keep their word.

If you say that you are going to do something – do it. Don't over exaggerate your influence and be sure to under-promise and then over-deliver. When you keep your word, you deposit into the trust bank account. The more deposits you make the more willing others become to help you out when you need it. They become your advocate who cannot wait to promote you to their network.

Again, the more trustworthy you are the more cheerleaders you are going to have and the faster your network explodes.

When you develop a circle of trust around you in your network; other people clamor to get into it. Your word is your bond – it means everything. If you can't keep your word, you might as well quit networking right now because all your efforts will be in futility.

Just think about how you feel when others don't deliver on what they say they will. Do you continue a fruitful relationship with such individuals or entities? Of course, not – even on a second chance to make good, we move very cautiously.

So, keep your word and watch your network explode beyond your wildest dreams.

Step #6: Stay in touch

One of the most important things you can do to maintain your network is to stay in touch on a regular basis. This takes effort and commitment, and you must be willing to do it in order to yield the best results.

Killer networkers are masters at follow up and staying in touch. Often times they tend to call unexpectedly but somehow right at the most needed times. So often I call people where they say to me "Dean, I am so glad you called me today. I really needed to hear that."

Not only does that feel really great to hear that you were able to make somebody's day but also, people remember these moments forever. They never forget what you did.

For instance, one of my great mentors has a wife that suffered a heart attack and stroke. Of course, this was an extremely difficult time for him. Now I don't know what his health plan is like, but I do know it's the best of the best just because of whom he is and where he works.

With that said, I could just see the toll this was taking on him and I could only imagine what his wife was going through. I didn't really know if, or how I could help him through this – I only know that I felt compelled to do something.

I didn't care about what he could and might do for me – I just really wanted to help.

In that vein, I decided to send him an e-mail that outlined an alternative health care regimen for individuals who suffer heart attacks and strokes. It cost me nothing but a little time since I am a member of Natural Cures network. I simply went to the website – looked up the info and sent it to him.

Needless to say, he has never forgotten this gesture, nor do I think he ever will. The bottom line is he is one of my biggest cheerleaders and if I ever need anything at all, all I have to do is pick up the phone.

Now, you might think to yourself that this was a calculated move; however, authenticity is key in these situations. My family truly does strive to live an organic, farm-to-table, process-free life, and we are constantly looking for alternative health regimens. What I sent to my mentor was literally a piece of my own life – it's how I care for my family.

The point is that regardless of what anyone might think – my gesture was genuine, and he knows it. That is all that matters.

So, I realize that staying in touch and seeking to help could almost be one topic; however, it is important to understand that by staying in touch you get more chances to find genuine ways to help others. This is the quest of all killer networkers.

Step #7: Ask for help

Of course, there is really no use having a vast network if you can't lean on them to help you achieve your own dreams and goals. There is absolutely nothing wrong with this.

It is only wrong when you use others to achieve your ends. In other words, if you only reach out to people for what they can do for you – that's called *"using."* On the other hand, if you truly reach out to others to help them, there is no shame in asking for help when you need it.

As a matter of fact, all killer networkers understand one very crucial thing about networking – you can't do it alone. Independence only yields good results; however, the greatest results are achieved through collaboration, Interdependence – **Synergy**.

There is nothing wrong with asking for help when you truly need it. Other people feel empowered and more confident when you seek out their help. You can do a lot for others in helping them achieve significant strides in their own personal growth by simply reaching out to them for help.

While you should never look outwardly for validation – it is always nice to be recognized for your true gifts and talents. When you ask others for help, it is another way of affirming their unique gifts. It is a great way to say that I appreciate you and I need your help to achieve my goals.

So, don't forget to ask for help when you truly need it – no one will be mad at you for that as long as you remain genuine.

Master these **7 Steps to Killer Networking Skills** and you will undoubtedly catapult your *networking skills* to heights unimagined. Killer Networkers know and practice these 7 religiously and the results they achieve are the proof in the pudding.

Secret #3: 7 Steps to Killer Negotiation

I have seen it explained in many ways and watched it happen on different turfs and more often than not, the posture and position are always the same. People mistakenly enter a negotiation thinking that someone has to win, and someone has to lose.

I know that the dictionary's definition of negotiation states that negotiation is a compromise, a concession, a series of give and take or finding the middle ground. Personally, I think that the dictionary is limited on this subject and is quite shortsighted.

There's more to a negotiation than mediocrity which is where you end up when you seek the middle ground. The middle ground is short-lived because people on one side or both sides harbor resentment for not having achieved what they set out to.

In my view, there is definitely a higher purpose in negotiation and that is to achieve the third alternative - **a win/win**.

A negotiation then, by the *Dean Forbes'* definition, is a synergy of two ideas, the beginning of a fruitful and long-lasting relationship; it is a series of give and give where the ends meet the desires of both sides.

Many people will say that this view is terribly optimistic and therefore unrealistic. BUT I beg to differ because I have had the experience of both, and I do know that win/win is always better than win/lose and that win/win is almost always achievable. And, even when win/win is not achievable, there is still a far better option than win/lose.

Think about this...

The number one reason that people stay too long in toxic relationships is that they either believe that they can change the other party or that the other party will eventually see things their way.

All the while not realizing that sometimes the best outcome is to simply remove yourself from the equation.

Sometimes a win/win is as simple as that – the decision to step out – to leave.

Let that sink in for a bit.

Following are the **7 Steps to the Killer Negotiation**. Study them and put them into practice; I guarantee that once you do you will discover how easy it is to consistently achieve the results you desire. You will see immediate and profoundly positive results in all of your relationships, both personal and business.

Step #1: Know What You Want

I realize that this first step is obvious and that you surely don't need lessons in it but in the spirit of being thorough, I'll cover it anyway.

You never know, they may want to publish this material in the "Dummies" book how to series.

Ok, where were we? Right... step one.

Before you enter any negotiation, you'd better know exactly what you want and why you want it. You need to have a clear mission before you move. Begin with the end in mind at all times so that each move you make will be focused and purposed in achieving your mission.

The clearer you are in your mission, the easier it will be for you to navigate a negotiation.

Knowing what you want though is more than just knowing your mission – you also need to know the why so that you can master the right content. Without the why, you won't know how to process the information surrounding your mission.

You will not be able to deliver your goals with clarity and precision. This means that you must answer the question of why you want what you want.

You should know how your mission will benefit others; you should understand the impact and its significance, and you should be able to clearly outline expectations. The last thing you want is to be surprised by any information you might learn during your negotiation – you must be prepared.

Step #2: Foresight is better Than Hindsight

Remember what I said at the end of step one about being prepared? Well, this is the step where you bullet proof your preparedness. You may have heard the cliché; hindsight is 20/20 BUT I like to believe that foresight is even keener than that.

With the proper research, your foresight could be a magnificent asset in any negotiation. Before you set foot at the negotiation table, make certain you go the extra mile on reconnaissance.

Find out everything you can about the market in which you are negotiating and know all you can about the other negotiating party. The more you know about the other party to the negotiation, the more you'll be able to offer.

Armed with this information, you can anticipate questions, concerns and objections and make the necessary adjustments beforehand to accommodate their needs. There is no icebreaker more powerful than providing what is needed without being asked. Performing recon duties will help you tremendously in opening up the other party to your needs.

They will view you as intuitive and considerate and whatever tension was expected to be in the room will have dissipated because of your foresight. Besides, what good is hindsight when the deal is behind you? You want to affect the deal while it's in front of you.

Step #3: Sit On the Same Side

Many negotiations start with the parties on opposite sides of the table. This is because most people view negotiations as a war between enemies, so they sit on opposite sides of each other. They see each other as opponents.

This is not an effective approach because it creates distrust from the onset and those walls become harder to break down as negotiations ensue. A more effective approach is to sit on the same side of the table.

This is not a war; you are not enemies and there is nothing to be gained in the others defeat. Instead of viewing the other party as an opponent, view them as partners seeking to help each other and work successfully together.

If you sit on opposite sides, the tone of the negotiation will be inflexible, standoffish, and cold. Conversely, if you sit on the same side, the negotiation will suddenly become a conversation between two parties with great respect for each other. You can share ideas and seek solutions without the BIG elephant in the room – no tension.

Sitting side by side removes the air of confrontation and introduces an air of camaraderie and cooperation. When you sit on the same side, it means no one is looking for a fight but you are looking for mutual and free exchange of ideas in order to reach the same goal – making each other happy.

Step #4: Understand What They Want First

This step is crucial in every aspect of your personal growth and it's an essential element of negotiation. This can be a hard step to grasp especially if you are an eager beaver and all you can think about is what you want.

In fact, most of the literature I've read on negotiation encourages this maxim – focus on what you want so you can convince the other party to give in.

This is not an effective approach. If you take the position of self-centeredness, you will be speaking to a closed audience. The other party won't be open to listening to you because they don't feel as if you've listened to them – they don't feel understood.

This is why you must seek first to understand what they want. This means you have to listen empathically to their desires, needs, goals and concerns. This is not an empty disingenuous portrayal of listening – you actually have to listen so you can truly understand what they want. You must show genuine interest and demonstrate authentic empathy.

Further to that, when you desire to truly listen, you will not only hear what is being said but also what's not being said, which oftentimes is even more important.

When you truly seek to understand, you do not simply listen with the intent to reply or just to go through the motions. You listen ardently with the intent to empathize and to help. At least for a moment, you suspend your agenda and exist only for the other party.

You should not stop listening and asking to follow up questions until you can clearly repeat to the other party exactly what they want and also what their main concerns are.

Only when the other party has concurred that they are satisfied with what you have understood from them should you move on. Once you can do that you will be able to clearly point out how what you both want will benefit them and help them achieve their goal.

Step #5: Reveal Your Vision

Once you've shown the other party that you understand their needs and goals, they will be more than willing to openly listen to what you want. Now is the time to courageously reveal your vision. I say courageously because even in the face of adversity, you must be willing to put your stake in the ground as long as you believe it will be of benefit to both sides.

Do not let what the other party said sway you from your mission... you can modify your delivery based on other events so far in the negotiations but the end in mind remains the same. Passionately and enthusiastically tell them your story – help them visualize why you believe this partnership can be a fruitful one.

Whatever you do, don't deter from your vision for the desired partnership. There may still be some elements that the other party objects to; however, you can work that out later. The point is to infect them with your fervent delivery – make them see what you see. The more clearly you can do that, the more open they will be.

Step #6: The Third Alternative

Chances are, depending on the desired goals and how effective you were through *step 5*, the negotiation could be over with both sides walking away happy. However, if there are still some things to fine tune, *steps 6 and 7* are essential.

The Third Alternative says that you can work together to come up with something better than what you both originally thought of. This means that one party comes to the table with one set of goals and the other with another set of goals that don't quite align with each other's expectations.

Instead of going for confrontation and win/lose, the third alternative says let's put our heads and our ideas together to create a better solution than what we thought of individually. In most cases this can be done without much pain.

Seeking creative solutions often bring out the best in people. You find that what you thought was important isn't so important after all when compared to something of higher purpose and value. Seeking the third alternative makes you highly flexible and adaptable and in so doing, no one loses, and everyone wins.

Step #7: No Deal is better Than a Raw Deal

What happens if you are unable to reach a consensus? What if there is no third alternative to be had? What do you do when the deal keeps breaking?

I am a big fan of *"Win/Win or walk away."* In other words, no deal is better than a raw deal. At some point you have to be willing to walk away. For me, that point is when one of the parties is about to walk away with the lose side of the deal.

I know that it may seem like a lofty goal to always achieve a win/win however, I do think it's possible and, in the cases, where it's not – I believe that the solution is to simply walk away.

Perhaps this is just bad timing. Why sour a budding relationship with a raw deal? At least if you walk away now, you leave the door open to try working together again later. If you allow one party to accept a raw deal, the relationship will be stagnated, and the fruits will rot before you are able to enjoy them. If a deal cannot be struck, walk away.

Do YOU Have What It Takes to Become an Effective Negotiator?

I don't know... do you? This is a question only YOU can answer for you. I wouldn't presume to make such a prognosis from where I'm sitting.

What I can tell you for sure is this...

It depends on what you consider effective negotiating. If you think that someone always has to win and the other has to lose, then you are off to a bad start.

Many people will and do disagree with my definition of effective negotiation; however, I can say with **absolute** clarity that these same people don't form long-lasting and fruitful relationships with the people with whom they negotiate – I have, and I do – even when we don't reach a deal, we can both be happy with the first time around.

So, if you want to answer the question honestly, first decide if you believe this approach is the right approach and then commit to living by the principles. Then and only then do I believe you will be able to master the **7 Steps to Killer Negotiation**.

One thing I won't tell you is that anyone can do it but I'm willing to bet that anyone as smart as you can do it.

Secret #4: 7 Steps to Building a Killer Team

Have you ever watched a high-performing team in action? Better yet, have you ever been a part of a high-performing team?

I don't know how many of you watched the show that the Chinese put together for the 2008 Summer Olympic Games, but I can tell you it was truly a spectacular sight and accomplishment. This was the pinnacle of a high-performing team in action – what I like to call a *Killer Team*.

The pure energy and masterful synchronicity were absolutely impeccable. They were fluid and flawless during every show and absolutely electrifying with every move. It was definitely a sight to behold and if you didn't have the opportunity to see it, I can say without a doubt that you missed something very special.

If you get the chance, just search YouTube for the opening ceremony and you will immediately get what I mean. Such a marvel has not been seen since and I don't know when we will witness one again.

I don't know what they will do when at the next Summer Olympic Games, but I do know they've got their work cut out for them.

I have had the opportunity to experience the difference between a Killer Team and a team that gets killed. It is always a much happier, more productive, more efficient, and more creative scene when you are on a Killer Team – as if that's not obvious.

It is so much more powerful that my ultimate goal when working with a team is to be a part of and cultivate a Killer Team. This is of the utmost importance the moment you begin to work in multiples.

Whether you are leading or are a part of a team, this should be your ultimate goal. Everything else that the team accomplishes rests with the way they are able to work together. It will be next to impossible to achieve any result of great value if your team is not working together.

If some of you are pushing while others are pulling, it will create negative energy and, in some cases, wreak irreparable havoc on the whole team. Contrary to the popular belief – opposites do not attract, especially when it comes to teams.

Like-mindedness is essential for team success; the goal of the team must be the focus of every team member in order to achieve the best results. Every person may have a unique gift, a different style and of course different personalities but everyone on the team must be of the same mind when it comes to vision, standards, and rules of engagement.

No one on a killer team is more important than the other; however, each person must know that their role on the team is important and puts the needs of the team ahead of any one individual.

Following are my lessons and experience on what it takes to build a Killer Team. I've broken it down into 7 steps that you can begin to apply immediately and achieve immediate and positive results.

Step #1: Embody the mission

So many people embark on new journeys, start new projects or new relationships without ever creating a mission for what they want to achieve. It is actually ludicrous when you think about it; see yourself in your mind's eye getting ready to do something without knowing the result you're after or go somewhere new without a map of how to get there. Imagine walking through life not knowing exactly what it is you are trying to accomplish.

Does that make sense?

Of course, it doesn't. That would only make sense to a moron, and I know that's not you.

So then, the first step in building a Killer Team is to embody the mission. Embodying the mission though means several things. In order to be one with your team mission, every member must be willing to commit to it without wavering; you must all see it through together.

Several things occur when a team has successfully embodied the mission.

Creating and living the mission – when the whole team is involved in creating the mission, it makes them feel like they are a part of something greater than themselves. Their values become a part of the whole which makes it personal and therefore automatically commands more commitment.

It is a lot easier to live a mission that you helped to create than to live someone else's that was created for you; in fact, I'd say it's damn near impossible to live a mission you didn't have a voice in creating.

This is absolutely essential if you want your team to fully embrace the mission – be one with it. You must all be involved in the creation of it and then you must all live it every single day for maximum impact.

Clarity in purpose – nothing beats the knowledge of destiny. When you know exactly what you want to achieve and precisely where you're going, it's pretty difficult to miss the mark. At that point you only have to choose the right vehicles to get you to your destination – to your goal.

A purpose-driven goal is one destined for success. Once every team member is clear on what the purpose is, expectations are aligned, and focus is singular. This creates power beyond your imagination and productivity skyrockets under these conditions.

I remember when I first joined the team at Hairdesign by Avantgarde, a multi-million dollar salon and spa in nestled in Southwest Florida. Although I had coached thousands of beauty professionals by then, this was the first time I was thrust into the owner's box.

Typically, I'd be the coach in came in once or twice a month for the day, train you, provided you with tools and resources for success and then my day was over.

But, as an owner, you now had the task of implementing what I taught and the oftentimes daunting task of following through on consequences and hard conversations. Most salon owners I has coached before this time dreaded these situations.

Nonetheless, here I was running this amazing salon and spa with my lady who had built one of the most successful small businesses in the industry – hands down. Still, it wasn't without its challenges.

One such chronic challenge was the cleanliness of the salon – we just had a hard time keeping people on top of cleaning. Some wouldn't do it at all, and others would end up constantly being everyone else's maids.

Not pretty, I can attest to that… sometimes it was downright ugly.

And then I said, enough is enough!

At the next team meeting, which we had once per month religiously, I brought up the cleanliness problem to the team and simply asked them how they felt about it.

Needless to say, there wasn't one person on the team who liked it but...

No one was willing to step up and own it either.

So here we are, a multi-million dollar gem, with high end clientele who have a very high expectation in their experience and yet, we were allowing something as routine and common sense as possible stand in the way of our next level success.

With that in mind, I asked the team what they wanted to do about it. There were tons of opinions about cleaning schedules, associates paying their dues, senior level gets to skate and on and on.

I quickly called a timeout and told the team the buffalo story. It goes like this...

On the plane of the Colorado mountains exists both cows and buffaloes. When a storm hits, you can see cows quickly running away from the storm as fast as they can and since they aren't very fast the storm would quickly catch up and beat them down.

Then they would attempt to run again, and each time get caught and beaten down over and over again until the storm subsided. What an agonizing way to deal with a problem, don't you think?

Buffaloes though take a different approach. Instead of turning away from the impending storm, buffaloes face it head on and run right through it. Sure, they feel some pain but only the one time. They just bite the bullet and get it over with.

And so, I said to the team, when it comes to cleaning, we have two choices, we can either be cows or buffaloes.

We either choose to go through the pain over and over again everyday until closing or, we bite the bullet like buffaloes and just get our cleaning done in the moment.

Which would you rather be, the cow or the buffalo?

Of course, everyone chose the buffalo. And from that we created the Buffalo chore chart for opening and closing.

Then we simply decided that whoever opens performs opening chores and whoever closes performs closing chores. And during the day, if you see something, do something instead of waiting for someone else to do it.

What really drove the clarity in purpose home though was that in that same meeting, we gave each other permission to point out when we observed any team member being a cow.

Now who do you think ever wanted to be singled out as a cow among buffaloes?

You guessed it... no one.

I won't tell you that all our cleaning problems completely disappeared;

however, I never had to address it on this scale ever again and our level of cleanliness and consistence who doing it skyrocketed.

When every team member is clear on the purpose and buys in, you have a high-performing team.

Roles & responsibilities defined – this cannot be stressed enough. I've seen so many teams implode because the members have no clue what each is supposed to be doing. This is what creates chaos on a team and breeds frustration that leads to conflicts that produce undesired or disastrous results.

It is absolutely imperative that roles and responsibilities are clear and that each team member knows not only what he or she is supposed to be doing but also exactly what each of the other team members are supposed to be doing.

This is important in order to achieve maximum efficiency and efficacy. It allows your team to execute at a high level with the least amount of effort. No double work!

One of the major reasons personal relationships fall apart is when there is a belief that everything needs to be 50/50. From that, you get the toxicity of scorekeeping and finger pointing when something goes wrong.

This happens while the most important thing is ignored – ROLES,

Everyone has gifts or affinities and when you combine that with the other party, you get synergy. But you need to define this up front so you can manage expectations and stick to your standards.

The greatest leaders know that they don't always need to be the smartest person in the room, but they surround themselves with smart people – oftentimes people they consider to be smarter than they are.

On a team it's no different – when each person knows and understands their role and what they are responsible for, you produce high quality results with speed and efficacy every time.

The tie that binds – this is what embodiment of a mission does; it creates a deep bond among those who've created and are indeed living it. This is a very important element as you will see in the next step, *Cultivate Synergy*.

If you create a mission together, live it daily together and commit together to see it through, this creates a powerful and almost unbreakable bond. It creates unshakable focus and through your commitment, it crystallizes your purpose – the team's purpose.

I still remember when I was blessed to lead the most incredible sales team at the largest beauty company on the planet. We were a team of 17 and we personified every step I'm going lay out here about building a killer team.

Truthfully, I'd say that my experience leading this team is what wrote the 7 steps I am sharing with you now – it was awesome. These guys are my tribe forever. I still get goosebumps thinking about all the success and fun we had on our 8-year journey together.

To this day, although we've all gone on to achieve incredible results in the next chapter, we still check in with each other from time to time. I love these people.

Step #2: Cultivate Synergy

Synergy is supremely important for any team to function at its peak. This is the pinnacle of togetherness in a common cause. When a team is synergized, each move they make is like flowing water; they move in fluidity and synchronized harmony. It's really a beautiful thing to experience and if you have, you know exactly what I am talking about.

Cultivating synergy requires transparency and openness among all the team members. It requires the desire to listen with the intent to first understand each other and also the courage to state your point of view with compassion.

It requires that, when trying to resolve issues or come up with solutions where not all agree, that you always seek The Third Alternative as you learned in secret # 1, 7 Steps to Killer Communication. This is a solution derived from all the desires combined to create a better solution than any of the individual ideas – it promotes and demands win/win.

Furthermore, cultivating synergy also requires that you cherish teamwork in all facets and eliminate competition – at least against each other. Competition among the team can easily, and often does, lead to *"I first and team second"* and selfishness. This creates the *"what's in it for me"* mentality which throws the whole idea of the team purpose right out the window.

Now look, I know it's natural for driven people like you to compete; however, to keep it healthy on a team, try leaderboards instead. Create an environment of cheerleading and empowerment. Encourage teammates to push the other to do better… hold each other up instead of tearing each other down. Use accomplishments as testaments to the possibility that you too can do what I have done.

That's real team spirit.

Rather than promote competition, Killer Teams promote collaboration; they promote cooperation and fellowship. Instead of sitting on opposite sides of the table, members of a Killer Team sit on the same side. Side by side is better than opposing sides – both from a physical and psychological standpoint. You might remember this premise from the 7 steps to killer negotiation.

When a team is synergized, trust is at its pinnacle – each teammate trusts the other to do exactly what he or she is supposed to do. Each member covers the other and is confident that his or her backside is covered at all times. If you are unable to trust your teammates, you will be unable to achieve success as a team.

Synergy is what made the L.A. Lakers of the 80's and Chicago Bulls of the 90's so great. The players trusted each other – they knew when to pass the ball to the next man and when to take it all the way.

They seemed to always know where each other was on the court and every man seemed to know where he needed to be in order to receive the ball and sink a basket. It was like watching beautiful choreography when these teams played.

I know I'd always want to be part of a team like that. How about you?

Step #3: Level the playing field

For the most part, every team has a leader as well it should. There should be someone in the director position – the person responsible for making sure the blueprint is followed and the goals are met. That being said, one of the most important elements of a Killer Team is a level playing field.

This means that no one and I mean no one is above the law so to speak. As a matter of fact, the first person upholding the laws of the team should always be the leader. His or her example should be like a shining beacon to all other team members.

Leveling the playing field is simple – it requires that every member of the team is accountable for his or her actions. Each person from the top down is held to the same standard and has equal opportunity to voice opinions, ideas, and grievances without fear of negative recourse. Each team member must treat every other team member as an equal and with love and respect.

Leveling the playing field in this manner can often create powerful and unbreakable bonds – it fosters loyalty. When every team member knows that his part is just as important and is given equal standing to the next person's, it becomes easy to commit. The purpose of the team comes alive and thrives in the harmony of collaboration – in synergy.

Just to be crystal clear about respect and equal standing…

Your standing on a killer team will always be affected by your performance and level of commitment to the team standards.

So, while you always enter on equal standing and with the utmost respect, it will only slip if you're not playing your part as you agreed.

In that case though, most killer teams would probably just cut you loose rather than going too far down the rabbit hole.

Clear? Great! Moving on…

Step #4: Foster heretics

Killer Teams are notorious for going against the grain – they often observe the masses and do the opposite. As such, even though a team usually has a leader, Killer Teams expect leadership to come from any rank, any position, anywhere. This is why they foster heretics.

Killer Teams are always looking for leaders – not just one. Heretics are leaders because they don't wait for others to make change, they start it, and others follow. Heretics abhor the status quos – they are not interested in the discovery from last week, they want to go forth into new frontiers and make the next discovery.

The best Killer Teams are usually made up entirely of heretics – leaders. Mindless sheep get left in the pasture while the heretics steal the dawn of the day. While you whine about breakfast, heretics are busy eating your lunch and stealing your dinner.

Killer Teams are known for beating others to the punch and the reason is that they only recruit innovative and forward-thinking individuals; those that would sooner crush the status quos than live a day by it. Killer Team members only like the status quos because it gives them a new challenge – it gives them a change to champion.

Killer Teams are at their best when they are fueled by heretics because there are leaders in every hall making changes and breaking new ground. When you are part of a team that operates this way, you are constantly in a state of inspiration because you see the world anew each and every day.

Step #5: Discourage conformists

As Killer Teams foster heretics, something else happens automatically, they discourage conformists. Conformists are those who uphold the status quos – they fight for the status quos. Conformists hate change, they consider most change a threat and that's why they live in fear.

Killer Teams have no use for these types of individuals because they know they won't bring any creativity or innovation to the table. They will simply do what others are doing without ever giving a thought to change; even in the face of a broken system, conformists will still fight for the status quos.

Go figure.

A team of conformists create nothing, build nothing, and change nothing. They simply do what they are told or what they are expected to do. There is a place for these people... in an ant hill. (Chuckles)

Ants are like programmed soldiers – they each have a job that they were born to do, and they do it until the day they die. That's great for an ant, probably get a medal or a crumb, but very sad for a human being.

As one comedian said of one of our presidents and I'll paraphrase, "conformists do the same thing on Wednesday that they did on Monday, no matter what happened on Tuesday." (Chuckles)

Teams that consist of conformists are the teams that are getting killed by Killer Teams. Conformists are managers, not leaders; they manage the assembly line and do exactly as they're told.

Heretics are leaders; they chase all that is considered taboo in the hopes of positive change. Killer Team members are heretics because they thrive on change and crushing the status quos.

My team, the one I mentioned earlier would never allow anyone to penetrate our armor of heresy. In fact, after the first time that I personally had to fire someone from our team, it was the last time I ever had to initiate it.

We didn't fire a lot of people in 8 years, probably three total; these were more like growing pains, and they happened early on.

My point is that for the other two that we had to release, that was a concerted decision by the team before I ever had the thought. They came to me and said, "hey Dean, so and so is cool but umm, he's not gonna work out, and here's why."

After they listed the "whys" I knew they were right because they had bought in completely to the DNA of our team, our way of life. The decision was easy to make although we never like to deliver bad news. In the interest of cultivating a killer team though, it was a no-brainer.

Step #6: Be A Square

If you want to build a Killer Team or lead one, you must understand and master how to be a square. Ever wonder why it almost always never works when a third party tries to solve problems in a relationship, especially when no request was made for help?

The third wheel is usually told to butt out! You may have experienced something similar before.

On a team, one of the worst things you can do is create triangulation in a problem. Triangulating a problem means taking a problem that occurred between and affected two individuals or two groups and inserting a third party to fix the problem.

What usually happens is, the conflicting parties end up confessing each other's sins and then the mediator is left in the difficult position of deciding who's right and who's wrong. This almost always never ends well – at least one person or one group typically comes out of this situation unhappy.

Individuals who build and lead Killer Teams never create triangulation in a problem. Instead, they promote one-on-one Third Alternative resolution. This approach basically says that if you have a conflict with another teammate, you agree to work through the issue together until you reach a resolution that you are both happy with.

If a third party is ever inserted into the equation, it would only be because the conflicting parties both agreed that it was best in the course of resolving their issue.

This even works wonders in your personal relationships.

I have two daughters who are considered Irish twins as they were born almost a year apart to the day. They are very close and growing up they've been best friends.

That doesn't mean there isn't conflict. I mean after all, they're sisters so you know there's going to be drama sometimes.

But from the time they were very young, their mom and I never solved their conflicts for them. We always empowered and encouraged them to talk it through until they reach a resolution that they are both happy with.

In the beginning, sure, we steered the ship just a bit to get them on the right track; however, they've always been able to come up with their own resolutions.

They don't have very many disagreements these days and we rarely ever hear of any conflicts because they know what to do. That's all possible because as parents, we chose to be squares.

I'm extremely proud of the young ladies they are, and I am confident that they will change the world significantly one day.

So, when you build and lead a Killer Team, you must commit to being a square with every team member, no triangulation ever unless explicitly requested by both conflicting parties. Be a square and you will always be fair.

Step #7: Get out of the way

Many teams have been thrown completely off track when this element gets muddled. It is possible to build and lead a Killer Team only to find that you've limited its potential by constantly getting in the way.

Any idea what I'm talking about here?

You know the old cliché of "if I want the job done the right way at the right time, then I'm the only one that can do it." Or "no one else is going to care like I do so I might as well do it myself."

Sound familiar at all?

Part of the reason for adhering to the 6 *steps* above is so that it makes it very easy for you to follow the **7th**.

Once your Killer Team is in place and every team member knows what to do, as a leader your job is to now get out of the way. When you remove yourself from every nook and cranny, remarkable things begin to happen.

Team members work together, creativity is high, and results are astounding. I've seen so many talented leaders fail at getting out of the way so badly that the team failed, and the mission never got off the ground.

I remember once when I was charged to lead a group of about 90 individuals at a company symposium. My task was to lead the team of individuals who were monitoring classrooms and catering to the customers.

This by far was one of the most important leadership roles at the symposium. On the morning of the pep rally just before the event got underway, I was scheduled to give my team a pep talk – prepare us for what was ahead.

I said many things that morning but one of the most important things I did was recognize the incredible talent that was on my team, plant the seeds of the mission and then stepped aside and watched a well-oiled machine run.

The results were, as you can imagine, astounding. I was confident in the tenacity of the team; I knew that it was packed with heretics and experience, so I simply shared the mission, gained unanimous consensus with it, and then provided a platform for them to execute – I got out of the way.

This is often very hard for leaders to do – instead, they try to control every outcome and every process. For the most part though, all they end up doing is managing instead of leading which defeats the entire purpose of building a Killer Team.

What kind of team are you on?

So, are you on a team? Where do you think your team falls, *Killer* or *Getting Killed*?

If you want to build teams that accomplish great things, you must be willing to commit to the 7 steps above. I realize that it may seem like you don't have much of a choice when it comes to who is on your team, especially if you have a job; however, you can still be a heretic, a leader.

You can start your own Killer Team within a team. Perhaps you want to start a Killer Team at work whose sole purpose is to create positive changes in the workplace and stamp out the status quos. Just remember, the top doesn't always mean the CEO, the top can start with you.

Secret #5: 7 Ways to Add Killer Value to Anything

If you ever wonder why some people are so good at what they do or how some of the top salespeople are making the numbers every day, this is a section you need to pay close attention to. Top performers have all mastered one thing – How to add **Killer Value** to their product or service.

Quick story...

There is a zoo in Denver that had a dilemma when it was just about ready to open its gates to the public. The management realized that the cost of removing the exotic animal waste from the property was not only going to be astronomical but also leave a big footprint on the environment.

Determined to find a better way, the leader of this team charged the entire management team with figuring out the best way to reduce the cost of this liability as well as make a smaller footprint on the environment.

No small feat if you asked me.

Nonetheless, the team went to work brainstorming ideas on how to make this happen. By the time the zoo opened, they had devised a plan and implemented what I believe was the most innovative solution.

*At this Denver zoo today, you can buy garden manure called Zoop; I'll let you guess which two words make up "***Zoop***."*

Essentially, rather than paying exorbitant amounts of money to haul away the waste and create all sorts of toxins in the environment, the management decided to simply package the waste in the form of manure to be sold as fertilizer to anyone with a garden. Needless to say, the lines are frequently out the door with patrons purchasing Zoop in droves.

Another zoo in Kansas City, MO repeated this same idea opting to call their product Zoo Manoo. Either way, this is definitely high on the scale of adding killer value.

The point is that if you can add value to animal poop, you can definitely add value to anything.

Let's dive right into the step-by-step guide to adding killer value to your product or service, assuming of course that people want or need it.

By the way, if you're the only commodity you're selling, it'll work for that too!

These are the **7 Ways to Add Killer Value to Anything**. The ability to implement any one or a combination of these ideas will instantly improve the value of your product or service even when that product (or service) is simply YOU.

Way#1: Bigger

Bigger refers to quantity; you can always do more of or make it bigger than the competition. If you want to outdo the other guy, creating a bigger fanfare or doing more of the same will instantly add value.

In this case size does matter and people appreciate it. There is a reason why those "All You Can Eat" restaurants do so well. It's not about the portion you get; it's about the value it adds knowing that you can eat to your heart's content for a very reasonable price.

In the case of adding killer value, BIGGER can definitely be a good thing.

Think Costco or Sam's Club.

Way #2: Better

Obviously, it would add value to your product or service if you can do it better than everyone else. Whatever it is that you sell or whatever service you provide, consistently seeking ways to do it better will instantly set you apart from the rest of the pack.

Better is about quality and research shows that most people will gravitate to other people and companies if they know for certain that the quality is better.

Certainly, many decisions are based on price; however, for the most part people will value quality over price especially if the product or service is within their budget.

Don't misconstrue the point here; I'm not saying that people will go out and drop their Honda to buy a Mercedes – not at all. I am saying however, that many people would rather go to Trader Joe's versus the mini mart on the corner because the quality of the foods at Trader Joe's is better and the prices are still reasonable.

Way #3 – Faster

Speed is definitely a plus in adding killer value; the faster you can provide something, the better. People love instant gratification so if you can find a way to deliver your product or service faster than the other guy, you're golden – your customers will love you for it.

Of course, your quality cannot suffer for the sake of faster delivery; otherwise, your purpose will be defeated.

Adding killer value with speed simply means that you are able to deliver the same or better quality product or service at a faster rate than your competition. Now that's killer value!

Way #4 – Innovate

Why you? How are you uniquely different from the other guy and why should I give you, my business? This is what it means to innovate; you must find a way to deliver your product or service differently.

This is where creativity comes in; innovation is how you stay ahead of the pack. When you consistently seek new ways to improve your product or service, the value is immediately recognized. You are definitely in a top class when you are able to do this consistently and successfully.

Way #5 – Exclusivity

Killer value is instant if you can find a niche and then figure out how to tailor your product or service to fit that niche. Keep in mind that the niche needs to be big enough to sustain your growth; however, once you have identified such a space in the market, you can easily begin to add value.

People love to feel special therefore exclusivity of any kind can carry extremely high value. Just like the Denver Zoo found a niche in exotic animal waste, you can also find a lucrative niche in your market.

The fact is that any animal waste can be processed to be used as fertilizer; however, exotic animal waste is more appealing to a certain group, and you have to visit the Denver Zoo to get your own ration of Zoop!

That is definitely exclusivity that adds killer value using several of the killer ways mentioned in this section.

Way #6 – Personality

You can always add killer value by making your product or service more fun or more serious or more creative depending on your target audience. If it's more fun to do or to use, many people will recognize that as instant value.

Chucky Cheese has made a significant impact in making children's parties more fun! You simply show up with all the children, eat the foods they provide and enjoy the fun activities available all for a reasonable price.

The best part is they do all the work including the cleanup which we all hate. If that's not adding killer value, I don't know what is.

It may seem simple but, it really does work. Why do you think Chucky Cheese has been so successful?

Whenever we entertain at home, the cleanup is always the most dreaded part. Each time we do, we always wish we had someone else to take care of that part especially.

Way #7 – Relatable

If you can make your product or service more relevant to your target, you can add instant value. The more you can resonate with your customers, the better. Identity is important and one of the most valuable things that any business owner can do is to find ways to relate to their customers.

Let me give you a few examples.

Nike once ran a campaign where not only could you purchase your favorite Nike running shoes, but you could also customize them with your name or any phrase you wished up to a certain number of characters. Now that is really taking relevance to another level. It's relevant only to you and no one else – they're special. Still have my pair after almost a decade.

*Google is the **KING** of relevance by far with their main product – the search engine. All you have to do is type in a keyword and the engine returns only those products and services relevant to what you want. The same goes for the advertising portion – you get to choose your customers based on relevance to your product or service.*

Cable service providers have this down to a science by creating specialized packages tailored toward different types of people. For instance, you might have a sports package, a movie package or a home and garden package. Depending on what types of programs you enjoy – there is always a RELEVANT package to choose from.

When you deliver your product or service in a way that speaks to the identity of your customers, killer value is instantaneous.

Here's the skinny...

If you're a business owner where you are unable to implement one or a combination of these strategies, perhaps it's time to consider selling or doing something else. If killer value can be added to exotic animal waste (POOP), you can add killer value to just about anything.

Don't be lazy, your customers deserve better and until you recognize that – you don't deserve more no matter what you think. All incredibly successful people add value all day – they consider it their responsibility.

You will hear me say this repeatedly to nauseum – to achieve killer success, all you have to do is find a way to create and deliver value to others through your unique gifts and impact positioning.

It is a simple concept to grasp so start grasping. I didn't say it was easy to do – just simple to grasp. If it were easy, everyone would do it – but then that would be boring and make for a dull world. The truth is I wish everyone would do it, but the fact is only 4% do

Where do you fall?

Secret #6: Top 7 Sales Killers

Whether you know it or not, we are all in the business of sales. It doesn't matter what you do for a living, we all sell products and/or services. One thing is for certain – we all sell ourselves. It could be to family, friends, colleagues and/or customers – it doesn't matter – we all sell ourselves daily.

You've probably already read the previous section of this master blueprint on the **7 Ways to Add Killer Value to Anything** so I thought it appropriate to also make sure that you understand the flip side – what absolutely can kill your efforts to add killer value.

The fact is that we are all killers – the only thing you need to figure out is which type of killer you are. Ultimately, you get to choose the type of killer you want to be.

Whether you believe you are a killer or not – carry on – by the end of this section I think you will have gotten a clear picture in your head.

Following are my best insights on the elements that undoubtedly will *kill a sale*. The information is derived from my years of experience in marketing, sales and training and developing people from all walks of life.

These are the **Top 7 Sales Killers.**

Sales Killer #1: Assumption

The moment you assume anything at all about a situation or a person, you've basically killed the sale before it has even started. Once you assume, you make an ass-et out of you.

If the desired result is to make the sale – add value to the situation or person – you won't be able to achieve that outcome effectively if you've already decided, what the situation is or who they are.

All preconceived notions must go out the window and you must come to the table with a clean slate. Your only goal should be to add value and create a new customer.

Whether you're selling a product or service or simply starting a new relationship wherein you're selling yourself – any assumptions will defeat your purpose. It will rob you and everyone involved of the relationship's full potential.

Sales Killer #2: Cluelessness

This goes without saying; people don't buy from individuals who have no clue what they are talking about. If you don't know your product or service and you don't know what the customer wants or needs, you're clueless and in their eyes – **USELESS!**

Before you attempt to make any sale, make sure you have all your information – your facts – straight. It is also crucial that you know the most relevant information about your customer. This way you can relate to him or her better – this is a key element in adding value. Simply put – you'd better know your stuff or end up getting stuffed.

In short – **GET A CLUE!**

Sales Killer #3: Judgment

Judgment is the brother of Assumption because it limits your range of thinking. It creates barriers to the sale when you come with preconceptions of any kind. Judgment though also takes another form that can be detrimental to a sale.

If your customers happen to use your competitor's product or service and you bash your competitor, they will see that as a judgment – like you're bashing them. Instead of judging, try overcoming the competitor's product or service by offering more, better, or faster service. Show your customers why doing business with you will benefit them more.

Any judgment of your customers or the products they use will diminish your standing in their eyes no matter how good your intentions are. You will not only lose the sale but most probably a customer for life.

Sales Killer #4: Insincerity

If your heart is not in the right place, how can you act in the best interest of your customers? Authenticity goes a long way in forging strong bonds of loyalty and respect. Insincerity will eventually rare its ugly head and that will seal your fate and kill the sale with that customer.

The fact is that people don't care what you know until they know that you care.

Unless you have your customers' best interest at heart don't bother attempting the sale. Even if you make one or two sales to one customer as a sheep in wolves' clothing – your deeds will soon come to roost and your reputation will suffer dire and irreparable consequences.

Sales Killer #5: Indifference

Indifference is about the lack of conviction in the products or services you offer. If you don't believe in yourself or what you do, why should your customers?

If you waiver or blow from one stance to the next without rhyme or reason, your customers will be wary and leery of your motives.

When it comes to being a killer salesperson, you cannot afford to be neutral; one of the reasons top salespeople do so well is that they are able to rally others to a cause. Your ability to do that will be significantly hampered if you are indifferent and your customers won't be able to trust your word.

Why should people do business with you? If your answer on one hand is six and half dozen on the next – you aren't saying much. That position is weak and only shows that you don't really care either way so long as you make a buck. The sale will die a fast and painful death because of your lack of conviction.

You may have heard the saying before "If you stand for nothing, you will most certainly fall for anything." That's no joke – you will undoubtedly kill the sale if you are indifferent.

Sales Killer #6: Dishonesty

If judgment is the brother of assumption, then Dishonesty is the sister of Insincerity. These two go hand-in-hand; from the moment you are insincere, likely, you are also dishonest. Once this demon is discovered, there will be no sale – EVER!

It goes without saying that in order to build a circle of loyal customers; they must be able to trust you. You must always act in their best interest, say what you mean and do what you say you will do. If you falter on this priority, your sales are doomed.

Surely, you may be able to make a few sales through your dishonesty but again – this will eventually catch up to you. The longer it takes to come back to you, the more severe the consequences will be to your business and to your reputation. Your reputation is all you have; it takes time to build a really good one; however, you can easily destroy it in the blink of an eye.

Once you have been dishonest and your deception has been discovered, you will be hard pressed to find your road back to your former self. Not only will you have killed this sale but also jeopardized future sales as well. What can I say – word gets around fast in today's world.

Just remember, what happens in Vegas doesn't really stay in Vegas. It stays on Facebook, YouTube, Instagram, and Snapchat.

Tread carefully.

Sales Killer #7: Doubt

If you don't believe it, why should anyone else? It is a very simple concept; without your belief in your product or service, you cannot be an effective salesperson. You will never be a top performer when you come from a place of doubt and disbelief.

Customers see through this thin wall very quickly and just as quickly they will take their business elsewhere. Doubt shakes the ground you walk on and causes those around you to feel insecure. If I do not feel that you are able to protect my assets or that you even know how to, I won't do business with you.

Don't sell or offer any product or service you would not use or give to your family to use. This is a great way to benchmark the products and services with which you align yourself.

Belief and confidence are of utmost importance when it comes to making the sale; you must be able to stand by what you say and do and be prepared to back it up.

There is no substitute for belief and confidence and once you exude that, your customers will feel it too. Either way - it's contagious.

There you have it...

These are the **Top 7 Sales Killers**. What kind of killer are you? One who kills the sale or one who adds killer value? I suggest you figure it out before your next sales pitch.

Secret #7: 7 Steps to Killer Success

My sincere goal here is to help you recognize your own unique gifts and discover how you impact others. And learning that to then find innovative ways to share them with the world. It is about helping you to understand that unless you discover your true purpose, incredible success will continue to elude you.

In short, mastering this success secret will help you to grasp, understand and master the other six success secrets in the most abbreviated amount of time.

This is your simple **step-by-step** guide on how to achieve **Killer Success**. This is the type of success that 100% of people dream of but only 4% actually do something about it. I know – you're used to the 80/20 rule which is still true; however, I want us – YOU – to aim for the *pinnacle of success*. I want you to reside in the top 4% and I'm sure you do too.

Achieving Killer Success requires a great deal of discipline, commitment, and determination. People who achieve at this level don't know what it feels like to quit; they persevere even when all the odds are against them.

They leave it all on the line in pursuit of a dream greater than themselves. They are completely purpose-driven and whatever they do, they put people first. This is how you achieve **Killer Success**.

Following are 7 steps to help guide you on your journey to achieving your own killer success. Practicing these steps will undoubtedly catapult your success to heights you have not yet imagined and then some.

Step #1: Start at the finish line

I know – it might sound a little strange to you. Why would anyone suggest that you start a race at the finish line?

This goes back to the doctrine of being a purpose-driven individual. When you know where you are going and how you intend to get there, most of your battle is already won. All you have to do now is execute the steps accordingly.

All people who achieve killer success understand how crucial it is to envision your goal before you take the first step towards it. Have you ever heard the term "keep your eye on the prize?"

If you can already see yourself at the finish line as the first person through the tape – your focus will be more acute. You will be able to execute the necessary steps much more effectively because you know exactly where you are going and how you plan to get there.

Usain Bolt, the fastest man in the world was a star athlete way before the 2008 Olympics where he set the world records for the 100M and 200M sprints. But he failed miserably in the 2004 games; he didn't even qualify.

This wasn't because he wasn't fast or not in shape; his mindset wasn't there. He could see himself at the finish line, as first through the tape.

If you watched the next three Olympic games after that, you would see that he ran like a man possessed, as if he were just going through the motions to claim something that was already his long before he set foot on the track.

This is the part of the process where you pinpoint exactly what it is you want to achieve and then see it accomplished in your mind's eye before it actually happens. This is called creating the vision; it centers your actions on the ultimate goal thereby making your every move relevant and purposeful in achieving your end.

Imagine what you want the people you love and know to say about you when you reach the twilight of your life; imagine the legacy you wish to leave behind for your children. Unless you have a clear picture of that, how will you know how to live your life accordingly?

The fact is that all people who achieve killer success begin every journey with the end in mind. This keeps you focused and on target.

Some people say, "I would love to change where I am"; however, the truth is where you are is the present and that you cannot change it because it is already here. What you can change is where you want to be BUT if you don't have an idea where that is, it will be hard to take the right actions to get there.

Step #2: Draw the correct map

If step #1 is where you create the vision, then step #2 is where you map it out. This is called vision-mapping. Once your goal – the finish line – is crystallized in your mind, you have to draw the correct map.

This means that you have to figure out what resources, tools, and people you need to help you achieve your goal. Drawing the correct map does not necessarily mean the fastest way to your destination – it means taking the right actions to achieve the results you desire.

To achieve killer success the correct map must be grounded in universal and correct principles. When you begin to connect the dots, it must always be for the right reasons.

Since this is your map, there is no reason you can't change it midstream as long as the change is grounded in correct principles. This means that on the road to your killer success, you must always put people first and things second; things you can replace – people you cannot.

The correct map also requires that you pay close attention to the signs on the road lest you get led astray. So often people start out on a road with one purpose only to find that by the end of the journey they've gone completely off course and the purpose they started with has been eroded.

Can you imagine trying to get to Denver with a map of Boston?

You'll never make it.

Again, your map may change and the different stops you make along the way may change; however, you must stay true to your purpose. Each step you take must reflect your vision – your ultimate goal.

Step #3: Employ the 4 quadrants

Achieving killer success requires – demands that you go all or nothing. You must be in it all the way with every fiber of your being. This is what it means to employ the 4 quadrants of YOU. Your heart, mind, body, and spirit must be as one on this course in order to achieve the results you desire.

If your heart is not in it then your reasons for pursuing this course will be muddled and blurred. Your vision will be unclear, and you will easily go off track. Your heart is where the correct emotions and deep passion come from to fuel your actions. If it is not in the right place, you've already set yourself up for failure.

Your mind is the source of creation and innovation; this is your source of creating the vision and connecting the dots. With your heart in the right place, your mind will unleash more creative and innovative power than you can imagine.

If your mind is not in it, your plan will certainly go awry.

Of course, without your body, you cannot take any action on the purpose your heart has given you or on the plan your mind has designed. You must be willing to act because without action, nothing will get done. Without action, your dreams will quickly become fantasies and your killer success will ultimately become killer mediocrity. Unless you get off your ass and, in the game, you'll never put points on the board.

Your spirit is what ties everything together; it is your essence – it is the energy that you release into the world. If your spirit is correctly grounded in your purpose, it will tell you that you receive what you believe. This is a universal truth, and your spirit must be in line with universal and unchanging truths – principles.

Without belief, there is no way you can achieve killer success. If you believe you can't do it, you are absolutely and unequivocally right. In the same vein, if you believe that you can do it, you are absolutely and unequivocally right. This is the *universal law of belief* – **you receive what you believe** and more in abundance. If your spirit is not in it, your vision will surely perish.

Individuals who achieve killer success understand that the 4 quadrants are imperative in order to achieve the results you desire. Work on aligning these with your goals and your success will multiply a thousand fold and more.

Step #4: Spread the wealth

Spreading the wealth speaks mainly to two universal principles – the *law of gratitude* and the *law of giving*.

The *law of gratitude* says, the more grateful you are for what you have, the more you get to be grateful for. With killer success comes a level of humility that makes you feel grateful for all that you have. In showing that appreciation you simply get more and more to appreciate, and life becomes rich in every way.

This is why you must give thanks every day for the relationships and success that you have in your life. If you do this genuinely, you will certainly receive more than you can imagine for which to give thanks.

The *law of giving* says that whatever it is that you want more of in your life, you should give more of it away. Often, people misconstrue what this really means. The first thought many people have is, "how can I give away money if I don't have any to give away?"

This is because they do not understand that money is just a byproduct of success – it is not success itself. When you understand this concept, you begin to realize that what you need to give away is not money per se BUT the wealth you have in your life.

For instance, you can give away love, knowledge, help, kindness, and a host of other things that cost you nothing at all. If you are creating and distributing value to others, the byproducts of your success will begin to show up in your life and if you want more of those byproducts then you can give those away too.

The *law of giving* says that the more you give, the more you will receive. The caveat is that you should not give with the expectation of receiving something in return – that is disingenuous. You must always give with the intention to simply give; to create and distribute value to someone else.

When you do this genuinely, the universe will and must respond to you in kind. You will receive more than you give in return. So don't hoard the wealth – spread it as much as you can. Do it willingly, happily, and only with good intentions and your killer success will certainly flourish.

Step #5: Pay it forward

In the same vein as spreading the wealth, killer success demands that you teach and mentor others in some way. Through the steps you take to achieve your killer success, there were resources, tools and most importantly people that helped you along the way.

Paying it forward simply means that you endeavor to do the same for others. It means that you help others avoid the pitfalls that you may have suffered on your journey. It means that you share your experience with others so that they might learn from it.

When you give in this manner, it will help you avoid one of the major pitfalls of success – GREED. Paying it forward will serve as a constant reminder that you did not do this on your own and that you have others to thank. You honor that memory by providing the same or better opportunities for others. You help others find their voice and teach them how to draw correct maps.

There is not a single individual that I know of who has achieved killer success that hasn't made it a point to consistently pay it forward. Some do it in BIG ways and others in small ways. Either way, they do it consistently.

Step #6: Value Principles

Unless you place high value on principles, killer success will continue to escape you. In all that you do, you must adhere to correct principles. The universe acts without emotion; without judgment. It simply responds to natural laws no matter what.

Have you ever noticed that the more down you are the more the universe works to keep you down? Conversely, the more up you are the more the universe works to keep you up – these are natural laws at work. They act in the same fashion no matter what others do or say. They are unchanging and universal truths – principles.

Killer success demands that you value and adhere to correct principles in order to achieve the results you desire. This is the secret that all killer successful individuals understand. It is the fuel that drives and maximizes the first five steps. Unless you value principles, you will eventually run out of gas and your quest for killer success will fall flat.

Step #7: Do what you love

This step should probably go without saying; however, as I often say – better to be thorough. There is no point in practicing any of these steps if the 7th is not a part of the regimen. Doing what you love will help to further ensure that you say and do things for the right reasons as you pursue your goals; it ensures your commitment.

Of all the examples I can think of there isn't a single person who has achieved killer success that isn't doing what he or she loves to do. This being said, it is easy to misunderstand what it really means to do what you love.

For some individuals, they do not or refuse to see how doing what they love will bring them success because they don't see its direct relation to making money. The truth is that the moment you are doing anything for money, the love is not for what you're doing – it's for the money. This is a sure way to derail your killer success.

Remember the heart in the 4 quadrants? You have to love what you're doing in order to find the true value in it and then endeavor to distribute that value. Believe me, the byproduct, money, will eventually show up and it will be more than you need. This again goes back to the natural laws – the universe will respond in kind.

Another way to view this is that while what you do for a living is not the thing you love or what you are passionate about – it must be the means to that end. In other words, you may choose to do one thing in order to create the space and the freedom for you to do another – to do the thing you love.

For instance, let's say you love to travel – you are extremely passionate about it. You love visiting different parts of the world and learning about new cultures. Let's also say, it's not necessarily something you want to use as a vehicle for creating monetary success, but you would rather keep it as your private dream. What do you do?

Well, it would be naïve to think that in this case simply doing what you love will bring you killer success. It may bring you success in your peace of mind and personal fulfillment; however, it won't keep a roof over your head or put food in your belly. This is where the other 3 quadrants come in to save the day – this is why you need them all.

Your mind will create an innovative way for you to share your other gifts and talents with the world and your body will execute the plan that will give you the monetary success you need so you can pursue your true love at your leisure. Once your spirit is in line with correct principles as you do what you do – you will reap the right results.

Doing what you love then simply means that your actions are grounded in correct principles and that the map you follow ultimately leads you to what you love to do. It may be that your map is all about doing what you love, or you have simply created a map that consistently takes you to what you love. Either way the goal is to do what you love.

When you begin doing what you love –
you will never have to work another day
in your life. This is a beautiful thing.

So, What Now?

Now that you've read through the Top 7 Killer Success Secrets, you're probably wondering… "What the heck do I do now?"

Remember the user's guide provided just before we dove in? I suggest you start there. The point of this master blueprint is not for you to rush the process just because you just soaked up all this information.

None of this will amount to a hill of beans unless you put the principles into practice and see results. The measure of your success will not be measured by how much of this you know but by the results you achieve because of having known these secrets.

In a nutshell…

Practice, **Practice, PRACTICE!**

One of my great teachers would ask "How do you eat an elephant?" And the answer is simple, one bite at a time. This is no different – take your time – enjoy the journey.

This master blueprint should remain a reference for you as you go through the process. Just apply what you've read in each section and evaluate your results. Only move on once you truly believe that you've got the success secret you're working on under your belt.

And please – have fun!

I wish you the very best in your success. I can't wait to see the impact you make and the lives you change.

I know you will be great.

Printed in Great Britain
by Amazon